Mr Greedy loves eating. His tummy always feels as hungry as two elephants. What do you think happened when little Miss Bossy decided that he was too fat?

ME AND MY TUMMY

as told to Roger Hargreaves

© Mrs Roger Hargreaves 1985
Printed and published 1991 under licence from Price Stern Sloan Inc.,
Los Angeles. All rights reserved.
Published in Great Britain by World International Publishing Limited,
An Egmont Company, Egmont House, P.O.Box 111, Great Ducie Street,
Manchester M60 3BL. Printed in Germany. ISBN 0 7498 0 00 X
REPRINTED 1992

A CIP catalogue record for this book is available from the British Library

Hello! I'm Mr Greedy.

Every night before I go to bed, I fill my tummy with as much food as possible.

But, it's no use!

Every morning when I wake up, my tummy feels as empty as can be, and I feel as hungry as a horse.

Well, actually, as hungry as an elephant!

Well, truthfully, as hungry as two elephants!

Take this morning for instance.

I woke up at six o'clock.

It was my tummy who woke up first.
The rest of me was fast asleep.

"Come on," he said to me. "Shake a leg!"

"I'm hungry," he added.

My tummy talks to me all the time!

You can't hear him, but I can.

I groaned, and got out of bed.

Six o'clock in the morning is much too early for the rest of me, but not for old Tummy.

We had our usual breakfast.

TOAST - 2 slices.
CORNFLAKES - 1 packet.
MILK - 1 bottle.
SUGAR - 1 bowlful.
TOAST - 3 slices.
EGGS - 3 boiled.
TOAST - 4 slices.
BUTTER - 1 dish.
MARMALADE - 1 jar.

"Bit stingy with the toast," grumbled Tummy.

That morning, as usual, I went shopping.

As usual, for food.

On the way home I met little Miss Bossy.

"You're getting very fat," she said, prodding me sharply in the stomach.

"Don't *do* that!" said Tummy.

"You need to go on a diet!" she exclaimed.

Tummy didn't say anything.

I think he was a bit stunned.

"Where are you going?" she asked me.

"Home," I replied. Home, incidentally, is Roly Poly Cottage.

"For lunch," murmured Tummy.

"I'll come with you," said Miss Bossy.

I didn't argue.

"Right," said Miss Bossy when we got home. "I'll make lunch! You go and read the paper."

So I did.

"Come and get it!" she called out.

So I went into the kitchen, and there *it* was!

My lunch!

"I don't believe it!" said Tummy.

"Be quiet," I said.

"What?" asked Miss Bossy.

"Nothing," I said.

Half a tomato.
A piece of cheese.
A glass of water.
One lettuce leaf.

And two minutes later, lunch was over!

Tummy let out one of his larger rumbles.

"I do beg your pardon," I said.

"Beg for food," Tummy muttered.

"I've locked up all your food," said Miss Bossy cheerfully, "and I'll be back later," she added, "to make supper."

"Quick," cried Tummy as soon as she had gone. "Back to town!"

"Good thinking, Tum," I agreed.

And we were back in town in the twinkling of an eye, or the cracking of an egg, or the sizzling of a sausage.

I zoomed into the Eatalot, my favourite restaurant, and hastily glanced at the menu.

"Four hamburgers, lots of French fried potatoes and a large steak," I gasped.

"With an egg on top," Tummy suggested.

"With an egg on top," I said.

"And a double milk shake," Tummy murmured.

"And a double milk shake," I added.

My fork, with a large piece of steak, four French fries and a large slice of hamburger, had travelled halfway from my plate to my mouth when a shadow fell across the table!

"Aha!" cried Miss Bossy, as she seized not only the plate, but the milk shake, and even the forkful.

Tummy let out a little moan.

And I went home.

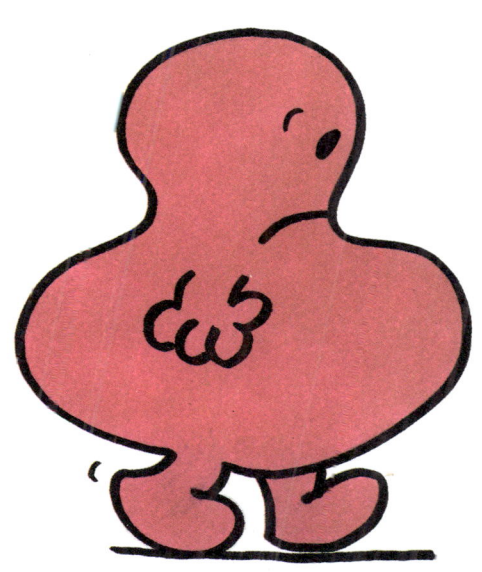

Miss Bossy arrived later in the day, and cooked supper.

What I was given was hardly worth mentioning.

So, I won't mention it!

It was, without doubt, the very, very, very worst day of my life.

Tummy and I went to bed.

"Cream buns!" whispered Tummy.

I ignored him.

"Chocolate pudding!" whispered Tummy.

I sighed.

"Vanilla ice cream!" whispered Tummy.

I whimpered.

"Smothered in raspberry sauce!" whispered Tummy.

I groaned.

"With a huge, fat, red, juicy, glistening cherry on top!" whispered Tummy.

"SHUT UP!" I shouted, at the top of my voice.

And that's what woke me up!

It was seven o'clock in the morning!

The whole terrible day had been a dreadful dream!

A dream?

A nightmare!

"Breakfast?" suggested Tummy.

"Be my guest," I grinned.

And we went downstairs for our usual breakfast.

TOAST - 2 slices.
CORNFLAKES - 1 packet.

And the rest.

I was about to pop the first hot slice of thickly buttered, and even more thickly marmaladed, toast into my mouth when there was a knock at the door.

"Don't answer it," said Tummy.

But I put the slice of toast down, and went to the door.

It was little Miss Bossy.

"You're getting very fat," she said, prodding me sharply in the stomach.

"Quick!" shouted Tummy.
"Lock the door!"